Go to page 47 & get your palate profile.

Love hanging out with y'all!

WINE SNOBS ARE BORING:

7 EASY STEPS
TO DISCOVER YOUR UNIQUE PALATE,
CHOOSE THE BEST BOTTLE
AND FEEL SMART
WHILE ENJOYING WINE
LIKE A TRUE HEDONIST

BY DALE THOMAS VAUGHN

CERTIFIED SPECIALIST OF WINE

D1365326

Foreword

Wine Snobs Are Boring

By Bryan Neustein, Wine Broker, Montesquieu Wines

Wine is a beautiful and complex thing. Its history dates back over 6,000 years, and is more revered now than ever. A ton of books have been written in that time on the subject, but I know of none that take the approach of this one. Most books assume you have at least a small amount of knowledge about wine. Whether it's verbiage, understanding regions, or having sipped a fair amount of wine. To truly start at the beginning, with zero knowledge, a clean slate if you will, offers an opportunity that becomes more rare the older one gets.

I have known Dale for several years and many bottles now. One thing is glaringly clear about him. His quest for knowledge is overshadowed only by his desire to help others realize that learning about wine can be easier than you think. You simply have to be willing to learn and get out of your own way.

I have been in the wine industry for a long time, and have drank my way through most regions and varietals. I always get asked two questions.

1) What is your favorite type of wine?

2) Can you recommend a good bottle that I might like?

The answer to the first question is usually "whichever one is in my glass at the time."

The second is the single most difficult question to answer. I don't know your palate, so it is difficult to point you in a direction.

To have a resource like this book is essential to taking the first steps to understanding your palate, and to not being intimidated by the thousands of bottles with all of the pretty labels and ratings at your local wine shop. Bottom line: does the wine taste good to you?

By not over complicating things and asking that one question, we can then start the learning process and have fun with the greatest alcohol delivery system of all. Regions, terminology, stemware shapes, food pairings, etc., will all come with time. Let's start with the first step, popping a cork, pouring a glass with friends, and seeing what is going on in the bottle. Because at the end of the day, isn't that the point of all this?

About Dale Thomas Vaughn

From humble beginnings pouring wine at an Olive
Garden in Texas to educating the Hollywood elite in
Beverly Hills, Dale Thomas Vaughn has helped thousands
of people discover their favorite wines and feel more
confident in the process.

(Photo by Ken Morris at CineGlitch.com)

With his P.A.L.A.T.E. system, he specializes in
converting beginners and wine haters into confident wine

lovers by identifying their unique palates and matching them with a varietal or region they've never tried. In the process, he shatters confining myths about wine and translates the esoteric jargon of the wine world into a language that normal people can understand.

He is a Certified Specialist of Wine by the Society of Wine Educators, a writer at the American Winery Guide for California's Central Coast, and a co-founder of a small backyard vineyard in north Texas. He has studied and traveled in France, Spain, Italy, Germany, Portugal, and the United States, specializing in the Santa Barbara AVAs of California.

His favorite bottle is always the one in front of him, but the ones that have stood out over the years have come from the Rhone, Loire, and Santa Barbara Valleys.

His methods are rebellious, intuitive, and candid.

Also by Dale Thomas Vaughn

Fatal Breach

Action/adventure in the Indiana Jones model. Arthur Haven is a man who finally gets his life together after a spooky incident at a Mardi Gras party where he is told he has 5 years left to live. It's about fate, purpose, romance, brotherhood, and holding on to the seat of your pants.

Dr. Mann's Kind Folly

One of the many stories I've written about Dr. Isaac Luther Mann, a time-traveling, jetpacking, mad scientist. This is actually a later story in his timeline (more stories to come), wherein he is forced to pause his grander dealings to help a child out of kindness... only to create an intense moral calamity.

Set in a future London with some H.G. Wells, Mary Shelley, and Jules Verne (steampunk) themes. I wrote it as a fairy tale - in fact as a reverse Pinocchio. There are A.I. robots, a tiny elephant and a talking falcon - so you know what you're getting into.

Connect with Me

Visit me at <u>www.facebook.com/DaleThomasVaughnAuthor</u>

or

<u>http://www.Twitter.com/NextGent</u>

Your Thoughts

I love hearing from my readers so please feel free to reach me and to leave a review here on my Amazon page:

www.amazon.com/author/dalethomasvaughn

Special Offer

Please see the back of this book for a special offer in appreciation for taking the time to read it.

Wine Snobs Are Boring

7 EASY STEPS
TO DISCOVER YOUR UNIQUE PALATE,
CHOOSE THE BEST BOTTLE
AND FEEL SMART
WHILE ENJOYING WINE
LIKE A TRUE HEDONIST

by Dale Thomas Vaughn

Published 2014 by Dale Thomas Vaughn

you, the reader. The contents are intended to assist you and other readers in your personal wellness efforts. Nothing in this book should be construed as personal advice or diagnosis, and must not be used in this manner. The information in this book should not be considered as complete and does not cover all diseases, ailments, physical conditions, or their treatment. You should consult with your physician regarding the applicability of any information provided herein and before beginning any exercise, weight loss, or health care program.

Front cover photo by www.learningDSLRVideo.com via Flickr

Back cover photo of author by Ken Morris via CineGlitch.com

Authors and sources cited throughout retain the copyright to

their respective materials.

For Elizabeth Menzel

It takes 3 years before a vine bears fruit

and 6 years before winemaking maturity.

Thank you for watching this slowly grow.

"In Europe then we thought of wine as something as healthy and normal as food and also as a great giver of happiness and well-being and delight.

Drinking wine was not a snobbism nor a sign of sophistication nor a cult; it was as natural as eating and to me as necessary."

Ernest Hemingway

Contents

Introduction

"I have a Wicked Allergy to Wine Snobs"

Dale Thomas Vaughn

This book is for you if you are, like me, allergic to wine snobs. Whenever one is around, I suffer from consistent and uncontrollable eye-rolling. Having studied wine for more than a decade, I know for certain that the more any rational person knows about wine, the more they learn they don't know very much at all. It's a humbling pursuit, at which mastery is so often the goal of the boring.

Snobs think their palates are somehow "better" than the rest of us mere mortals, which is total bunk. Having served thousands of glasses of wine to people varying from virginal to vertiginously above my level of technical knowledge, I believe fundamentally that every palate is its own filter for an experience. It's totally possible that the "best" wine in the world won't be exciting to you simply because it doesn't match your palate.

That's where this book will be different. This book is a somewhat rebellious, definitely precocious guide to unlearning the myths and misperceptions that may have held you back from experiencing the deepest pleasure, the widest outstretched freedom, and the sweetest sense of thriving that can come from the self-confidence given by the grapevine.

This book is about you.

This book is about the tangible tactics of wine, you will learn what you like, how to get the most out of a tasting experience, and you will learn answers to those questions you sometimes feel foolish for Googling after a run-in with a snob.

It's also about the deeper truth that you can learn all the wisdom in the world if you can just get past the woulda-coulda-shoulda kind of life. Yes, I'm serious. Also, I'm not serious. This is the nature of all things, and when in doubt I will always look to nature for a guide.

Chapter One - My Story

"Good wine is a necessity of life for me."

Thomas Jefferson

I grew up in a family of rural suburban middle American values and aesthetics with one distinctive exception... we took a lot of road trips. The family vehicle always had four wheels and enough gas to get us to a relative's house outside of our little bubble. Sometimes we went far afield, sometimes we were only whisked a few hours down the road; but we were always sure to get a little adventure, a visit with people who made us feel like honored guests, and a chance to try life in someone else's green pasture. It was a humble, sincere way to explore the world and experience new things. This was excellent preparation for traveling in wine country later in life.

Neither of my parents were connoisseurs, but they weren't teetotalers either. This last fact would turn out to be pivotal in my story.

During my college years I had a summer job waiting tables at The Olive Garden in Arlington, Texas. You may not know this, but The Olive Garden has a highly regarded server-training program that lasts a full week and includes tastes of everything on the menu.

It was during this training that I had my first lesson on wine. Mixed together with a bit of history and some corporate imagery depicting Tuscany... it was a seductive moment in my burgeoning worldview. That night I took the wine list home and talked my parents into buying a bottle of each from the liquor store - you know, for research. They were supportive of this endeavor and after my first in-house wine tasting I have been intellectually committed to this field ever since.

Has my palate changed since first being bedazzled by unctuously sweet and light-hitting wines like Chateau Ste. Michelle Riesling and Sutter Home White Zinfandel? Yes, undoubtedly. Therein lies the point. At any moment along the journey of your palate, you may find different levels of quality that are enlightening.

HISTORY NOTE

White Zinfandel is not white, it's pink.

If anyone ever gives you a hard time about drinking pink wine, remind them that for thousands of years wines were mostly all pink and easy to drink.

In French, "Rosé" means pink... thus pink wines are usually called rosé. Because most healthy grapes produce wine juice, the color in any wine comes from the wine fermenting with the skins and pits of the crushed grapes. White wine is juice that does not (mostly) have contact with the skins. Red wine does ferment with the skins. And Rosé juice is in contact with the skins for only part of their fermentation.

There are only a few places where red and white wines are blended to make pink wine... one of which is in Champagne where certain houses make sparkling rosés.

The next summer, I studied abroad in Cannes, France. On a road trip with the class, we stopped at a vineyard and chateau in the Rhone region of Chateauneuf-du-Pape. The winemaker invited us into his house at the Domaine de la Solitude and told us about the 800 year history of the vineyard, stretching all the way back to the popes of Avignon and the Schism of the Roman Catholic church.

HISTORY NOTE

For about 80 years in the 14th century the seat of the Holy Catholic Church was NOT in Rome, but was actually in a southern French town called Avignon. These Popes were said to be lovers of wine from Burgundy and from the surrounding region.

They erected a new castle in Avignon that housed the Papal court during the plague, and eventually the wine from the region became known as "vin du pape" or "wine of the pope." Sometime between the mid 14th century and now, the wine region became known as "Chateauneuf-du-Pape" in honor of the "new castle of the Pope."

The area is now famous for a blend of red varietals commonly known as the "Rhone-blend" of Grenache, Syrah, Mourvedre (and as many as 10 more grapes)... and was sort of rediscovered by the world after the fanaticism of a certain reviewer from The Wine Advocate now known to the world as Robert Parker (a name you'll need to know if you want to sound intelligent when talking about wine, he's the guy who basically invented the 100 point scale for reviewing).

I peppered him with questions that must have sounded incredibly basic to this noble winemaker, but to his credit, he never made me feel silly or idiotic. He instead invited the questions, gave freely of his knowledge, and I could sense he was honestly excited to share with someone who cared so deeply about his life's work.

After the rest of the students had been sufficiently bored by my incessant questions, they all turned to walk among the vines while I stayed behind and was treated to a special tasting by the winemaker. He pulled out a dusty old bottle without a label and he poured me a glass. I'll never forget the smile on his face. He was pouring magic into my life and hoping I understood the significance of the gesture. That single taste changed my entire perception of wine, of possibilities, of beauty, of artisanal mastery... of life.

Chapter Two - A Backwards Way to Learn Wine

"Language is wine upon the lips."

Virginia Woolf

In the inherently flawed but incredibly informative course guide for L'Academie du Vin, Stephen Spurrier (you might know the portrayal of Mr. Spurrier from the wine film about the 1976 Judgment of Paris: Bottle Shock) claims there are two different styles of tasting: the **technical style** and the **hedonistic style**. I'm obviously a big fan of the latter, though I admit a level of mastery of the former can increase the pleasure derived from wine.

He also admits they often cross over, and his coursework is founded on the very belief that an academic pursuit of understanding wine is both enjoyable in and of itself, and also enjoyable as a sort of bonus skill set for hedonistic tasting.

I wouldn't dare disagree, but I would postulate that it is challenging to walk the line between academic pursuit and intellectual snobbery when introducing wine to a neophyte. In my experience, the easiest and most entertaining way to learn wine for anyone from novice to intermediate is all about moderation.

I'd also add that general wine production knowledge isn't really necessary in the beginning of your journey with wine. I'll argue that the way wine has been taught for a century is exactly backwards.

If you take Mr. Spurrier's course, you'll learn generally about the vineyard and wine production first, then about the important regions, then about the grapes (varietals), and then at the very end... how to taste wine well. On his first page, indeed in his first sentence, Mr. Spurrier asserts that you need to know how to identify wines based on French wine laws in order to get the most out of his course. While I personally find wine law to be intellectually stimulating (especially as a backdrop for historical narrative), I don't think it makes a real difference in any experience with tasting wine.

So I came up with the PALATE method to learn wine for beginners.

If you had time and you were at my bar, or sitting at my dinner table, I'd start by helping you to discern your **Palate** (Chapter 3) and what you will probably like, then I'd help you **Ask** all of the most common questions about finding, buying, storing, and caring for wine (Chapter 4), then I'd help you learn how to actually **Love** the act of tasting the wine in your glass (Chapter 5), then I'd help you make a plan for your **Adventure** through new wine regions and grapes (Chapter 6), then I'd get into the **Technical** aspect of winemaking (Chapter 7), and then I'd talk to you about how to get further **Education** if you really wanted it (Chapter 8).

This is basically the way I learned wine over about 12 years of trial and error... just condensed and served to you in safe, approachable chapters.

Instead of being bullied by the "experts" through ratings, reviews, and even by the availability of a relatively small selection of variety... you get to skip forward and confidently stride to the bar with a grape and region that will make the sommelier behind the bar shake in his loafers because you know what you like before he can tell you what he thinks you should like.

The PALATE Program

1 Palate

Your unique palate is as important as anyone else's.

2 Ask

Learn how to ask questions to get and learn what you like.

3 Love

Discover how to love the wine in your glass in the moment.

4 Adventure

Plan how to explore the areas at the edges of your map.

5 Technical

The technical side of tasting and understanding wine.

6 Educate

Find where you can learn more about wine... if you want to.

I can't count the thousands of glasses of wine I have served to people over the past dozen years who initially said something like, "I don't like wine." After using my PALATE Program, I'll pour them a taste of something completely different than anything they've ever tasted... and they'll be converted for life.

But listen, I have a lot more to learn, and I'm certainly not acquainted with every single vineyard or vintner in the world. I will be candid with you throughout this book and program, and I expect and encourage you to find multiple ways to research and grow in your journey of the vine. This, I hope and believe is an excellent catalyst for that search.

Chapter Three - P is for Palate

Identifying Your Unique Palate

"Wine makes daily living easier, less hurried, with fewer

tensions and more tolerance."

Benjamin Franklin

One of the joys of my life is introducing people to their own palate. Over the years I've perfected the Palate Identity Program that has helped hundreds of people learn about their own palate by answering a few non-wine-related questions. You will get a chance to go through this program right now and determine the identity of your palate.

45

Answer the following two questions, after which you will be given a Palate Identity number and a profile... The Index has a comprehensive list of wines you'll want to try.

Once you have your Palate Identity, you will have all of the secret code words you will need to get the bottle of your dreams. You'll have a map of places to explore and grapes to seek. You'll know how to describe yourself with confidence when you approach a bar, restaurant, or pesky wine snob at a party.

You'll have so much vino-confidence that you'll quickly learn how boring all of the wine snobs in the room are.

Sound good? Ready?

Give yourself a rating on each of the following pages... and remember, just because there are numbers, doesn't mean there are grades. No one palate is better than another, so answer as honestly as you can and see what happens.

	Question 1: How do you take your coffee/tea?		
10	I Don't Like Coffee or Tea		Why be bitter when I can be sweet?
20	Caramel Frappuccino	Green Tea Smoothie with sweetener	I like coffee ice cream and tiramisu, does that count?
30	If coffee, 4+ spoons of sweetener and half-n-half	Sweet Tea	I can make coffee or tea work for me, but I'd prefer a soda
40	Frappucino, but no flavoring	Long Island Iced Tea	Cold and fun to drink is best for me
50	Mocha Latte	Mint or Green Tea	I like layered flavors - coffee or tea both need complimentary layers
60	Latte	Two Packets/spoons of sweetener	Sweetness isn't as important as softness, temperature and color
70	Cappucino	Iced Tea no sweetener	Dash of Almond or Coconut Milk
80	A little cream	Macchiato	You should see my fancy Tea collection - Yerba Mate, white tea, ginger... you name it
90	Espresso	Black Tea	Does Espresso Stout count?
100	Black Drip Coffee from a diner if possible	Turkish Coffee	I drink lukewarm Mud for breakfast, fear me

Question 2: What is Your Favorite Fruit/Flavor?	
10	Cotton Candy or a donut
20	Vanilla Cake, Vanilla Ice Cream
30	Mango/Citrus
40	Honey/Wildflowers/Lychee
50	Apple/Pear/Peach Cobbler
60	Red Berries
70	Pistachios, Roasted Nuts, Fresh Bread, Banana
80	Grape/Plum/Raisin
90	Bitter Dark Chocolate/Cranberry
100	I drink coffee for dessert

Now add up your total scores from question 1 and 2, and you will have your PALATE IDENTITY number. Next you will find all you need to understand about your palate to begin or enhance your journey into wine.

The Palate Identity Profiles

Total PALATE Score = 1 Through 40

Flavor Profile: "Sweet, and/or Floral"

Sweetness and softness are beautiful. You get bullied out of wine stores and into punch lines despite the fact that there are fantastic wines in your taste profile. There's nothing wrong with sweetness in life, and you don't know why everyone gets dramatic about this stuff. In some cases, you may feel either ashamed or defensive about your preference with wine. It's okay to be you! Own it!

Body and Mouthfeel: Soft, Light

Regions/Styles: Beaujolais Nouveau, Vinho Verde, cold weather regions like Austria, New York State and Germany, Lambrusco, Sauternes, Ice Wine

Grapes: Sweet Riesling, White Zinfandel, Muscat, Albarino, Viognier

Total PALATE Score = 41 Through 80

Flavor Profile: "Citrus and Floral and Bubbly"

You prefer wines to be refreshing and vivacious. You like the idea that wine is really just grape juice. You can get left off of wine lists or forced into drinking boring whites when you know there is so much more to your palate. You smell flowers and baking bread before anyone else, and when you drink a light red you can feel the sunshine straight from the grapes. If the wine list is boring, you'll just have a cocktail – but don't give up on your palate. Some of the world's best wines fall into your range.

Body and Mouthfeel: Light Red to Medium White, and almost anything Sparkling that isn't Bone Dry

Regions/Styles: New Zealand, Austria, Champagne

Grapes: Pinot Noir, Sauvignon Blanc, Viognier, Picpoul de Pinet, Pinot Grigio/Gris, Riesling, Gewurztraminer, Gruner Veltliner

Total PALATE Score = 81 Through 120

Flavor Profile: "Minerality, Berries on the Nose"

You like subtle power and simple genuine joys. You love the smell of freshly cut green gardens and rain on pavement. You are the reason why Chardonnay is such a big deal. There are all kinds of wines, all kinds of white wines, and all kinds of Chardonnay (Burgundy, California, South Africa, etc.). This one grape can taste like tropical fruit, minerals, or buttered bread – all of which you like. You'll need to find out your Chardonnay style. Butter usually means aged in oak, mineral usually means unoaked, and tropical fruit usually means young and unoaked. You will also find Sauvignon Blanc, Riesling, and

Chenin Blanc are good fits, and let's not forget pink and red wines – which you will love just a tad chilled and from a cooler climate. Head to a tasting room or bar and ask for a Chardonnay flight with three different styles... you'll find the one you love and will forever be an easy fit for the wine world.

Body and Mouthfeel: Full Body Whites and Medium Bodied Reds

Regions/Styles: French Rosé, the Loire Valley, Oregon, Washington, Germany, Chianti, Sherry, South Africa

Grapes: Pinot Noir, Sangiovese, Gamay, Chardonnay, Sauvignon Blanc, Dry Riesling, Picpoul de Pinet, Chenin Blanc

Total PALATE Score = 121 Through 160

Flavor Profile: "Complex aromas"

You are pretty happy with any bottle that hits your table. Of course you have preferences, and they are usually for anything that tells a story. You like layers and complexity and aged wines. You already feel confident in a wine situation because you can find something good about every wine, but what you live for is the moments on the frontier of your experience.

You are who wine tasting rooms are made for... explore any unknown wines and regions listed below and you'll find a new experience is still out there. You like the texture of mushrooms, the smell of grilled onions and the experience of an interesting cheese plate. You tend to prefer bourbon more than scotch and tequila more than gin. You are great on road trips, you make a good dance partner, and you have at one point or another loved roller coasters (this is me telling a joke).

Body and Mouthfeel: Anything with Good Body

Regions/Styles: Rhone Valley (France), Burgundy (France), Tuscany (Italy), Santa Barbara and Paso Robles (California), Russian River Valley (California), Mendoza (Argentina), Rioja (Spain), dry Champagne (France)

Grapes: Zinfandel, Syrah, Grenache, Barbera, Tempranillo, Sangiovese, Aged Pinot Noir, Blaufrankish, Malbec, Oaked Chardonnay, Loire Sauvignon Blanc, Chenin Blanc

Total PALATE Score = 161 Through 200

Flavor Profile: "Hints of fruit and lots of Earthiness"

You like depth, you like darkness, you like challenge... we're not talking about life, we're talking about taste. You will always be the one at the table who asks to pass the pepper. You like steak, blackened fish, and bacon. You don't understand why some people prefer milk chocolate over dark cacao chocolate. You love to meet people who can drink stouts, scotch, and port. The wine world is set up to make sure you have a wine on every list for you, and so you don't really have to worry about understanding wine as much as you have to worry about understanding which expensive wine is best. Go big, but don't always go home... in other words, there are fantastic bold wines from many regions, so make sure to try Piedmonte and Australian Shiraz if you're tired of Cabernet Sauvignon and Merlot.

Body and Mouthfeel: Robust, Jammy

Regions/Styles: Napa/Sonoma (California), Bordeaux, Italian B's (Barbaresco, Barolo), Australian Shiraz, dry Champagne (France), Sherry, Port

Grapes: Cabernet Sauvignon, Merlot, Nebbiolo, Syrah/Shiraz, Malbec, Pinotage; Aged Chardonnay, Riesling

You now have a Palate Identity number and profile, keep this in mind as we go forward. This simple profile can unlock the entire wine world and experience to you. In the next chapter I'll teach you how to employ this new knowledge in real world situations, and I'll answer all of the most frequently asked questions about wine so you can feel confident while you ask yours.

Chapter Four - A is for Ask

How to ask for what you want, and the answers to the

questions you have always wanted to ask, but didn't.

"Nothing more excellent or valuable than wine was ever

granted by the Gods to man."

Plato

You now have a Palate Identity number and profile that tells you how you like your body, flavors, and some regions and grape varietals you'll want to ask for at your next opportunity… but how exactly do you make sure you're getting what you want? You'll need to ask the right questions.

This can be scary because you've been bullied into thinking there are stupid questions. Below is a list of the most commonly asked questions about wine, and their answers. You'll find you probably know a lot of them already, but you'll also find some fun answers to the questions that have stumped you for years.

Before we get to those questions though, it's important to note that wine culture has certain vocabulary that is completely esoteric. You can either cower in a corner at the sound of lingo like "robust, jammy, oaky, or acidic;" or you can get in the game and make your own words up. This is a medium based entirely on sharing personal perspective, so take creative control and see if you can enjoy the interplay of making up your own sensual language around wine.

When asking for a wine to suit your palate, start by using some of the identifiers from your Palate Identity number. If you're a 150, say something like, "do you have any complex reds with good body and maybe some age on them? I like Rhone blends and Burgundies, but I'm also open to Zinfandel, Malbec, and Rioja." You'll knock the bartender over. Seriously. You'd be surprised what asking for what you want can do for you.

If the pourer comes back with something outside of what you specifically asked for, you can feel free to quiz him/her on the qualities of the wine. This is a great way to learn new things about wine, and a great way to feel confident while doing it.

As an exercise, write down a fictional conversation with a sommelier or wine store snob wherein you state what you want and then get to feel empowered and in control of the situation. Use your Palate Identity number to help you with your opening line.

The Most Commonly Asked Wine Questions

These questions were carefully collected from multiple websites and by polling my wine snob friends about what they usually get asked. I've collected them into relevant categories to help you have a cleaner and more direct approach to understanding them.

Is Wine Good for Me?

In moderation, wine has multiple health benefits.

Not least of importance, wine filters water. Alcoholic beverages have been invented in almost every ancient culture on Earth because of the lack of safety in drinking water. Water breeds bacteria and communicable disease easily without proper filtration, which is where beer and wine first came to prominence. Generally speaking, if you travel, wine is always more safe to drink than local water.

If you are fortunate enough to live with clean water (unlike 780 million people on this planet according to WHO/UNICEF), and death from drinking water is not among your top concerns (unlike 3.4 million people who die from water-hygiene related causes every year); then what you may be asking is more like health-related justification points for drinking wine, so you can feel good about the glass in front of you, or so you can argue with your crazy in-laws.

In that case, here are the ways wine has been proven or suggested to benefit your health:

In general, several authors have reported that in subjects consuming wine in moderation the risk of mortality from all causes is 20-30% lower than in abstainers.

According to several authors, moderate consumption of wine is more beneficial than that of beer or spirits.

Resveratrol might be a key ingredient in red wine that helps prevent damage to blood vessels, reduces low-density lipoprotein (LDL) cholesterol (the "bad" cholesterol) and prevents blood clots.

Neither the American Heart Association nor the National Heart, Lung, and Blood Institute recommend that you start drinking alcohol just to prevent heart disease. Alcohol can be addictive and can cause or worsen other health problems.

Drinking too much alcohol increases your risk of high blood pressure, high triglycerides, liver damage, obesity, certain types of cancer, accidents and other problems. In addition, drinking too much alcohol regularly can cause weakened heart muscle (cardiomyopathy), leading to symptoms of heart failure in some people.

HOW MANY CALORIES ARE IN A GLASS OF WINE?
Between 110-130 calories per glass (5 fl oz)

HOW MUCH ALCOHOL DOES A GLASS OF WINE CONSTITUTE?
Alcohol is usually measured in grams or fluid ounces, depending on the country. All pretty much agree on the "alcoholic units" measurement. Usually your bottle of wine will tell you the percentage in the bottle, this will help you calculate what's in your glass. A 12% bottle of wine has about 9 units of alcohol. A 16% bottle has about 12 units. So most bottles will be around 10-11 units of alcohol.

If you're out at a bar or restaurant, they will tend to overfill, likely giving you a glass with 3 units of alcohol.

Whereas if you're at home, you want to sort of stretch that bottle out among your friends and family, or for a meal... you probably only have 2 units in your glass at home.

It usually takes an adult about one hour to metabolize one unit of alcohol (give or take).

Most health studies recommend 2-3 units per day per adult, depending on body mass and liver function. Yes, that means about one glass per day is the recommended level of "moderation."

WHAT ARE SULFITES?

Very simply, sulfites are a preservative. Sulfur stops bacteria and other yeasts from growing, most often used to curb a second fermentation in the bottle. Secondary fermentation creates bubbles in a bottle, since the two products of fermentation are alcohol and carbon dioxide. Done on purpose, like in Champagne, France, it's delicious and delicate. Done on accident, it can cause effervescence in wines that don't go well with bubbles.

DO SULFITES GIVE ME A HEADACHE?

There is about 5 times as much sulfur in French fries as in your French wine... so sulfites probably aren't going to be an issue for you. However, if you are asthmatic, about 5-10% of people with asthma have been found to be severely sensitive to sulfites... check with your doctor if you think this is you.

"Sulfites can cause allergy and asthma symptoms, but they don't cause headaches," says Frederick Freitag, associate director of the Diamond Headache Clinic in Chicago and a board member of the National Headache Foundation.

WHY DO SOME WINES GIVE ME A HEADACHE?

The most common reason for headaches while drinking wine… is alcohol.

The research from Medical Wine Interest and Education Society in San Diego suggests that excluding alcohol as the culprit, the true headache triggers in wine might be histamine and tyramine.

Elizabeth Holmgren, director of Research and Education at the Wine Institute, suggests you drink in moderation and with food, and that if you're sensitive to histamine, consult your doctor and take precautions. Some doctors and researchers say taking antihistamines, ibuprofen or aspirin before you drink is effective in preventing headaches.

Also, Vitamin B6 can help your body metabolize histamine, some say. But, remember, some people can have harmful reactions to the use of these over-the-counter drugs with alcohol, so ask your doctor first. Drinking plenty of water when you're having wine might also help. Dehydration can cause headaches, too.

Choosing the Best Wine For You

WHICH WINE SHOULD I CHOOSE IN A RESTAURANT?

This is tricky. You want a wine that's going to fit a few different palates, you don't have a lot to go on, and you have a limited selection. People are getting different plates, and what you decide might even dictate what they will eat.

In this situation, I usually go for a medium bodied red that is likely to have some fruit-forward notes and decent alcohol content. What you don't want to do is blast the bitter tannins (unless everyone shouts that they LOVE Cabernet) or accidentally pick a sweet wine (if you don't know Rieslings and the server can't tell you it's definitely dry... steer clear). You're probably looking for a decent

Rhone, Burgundy, Santa Barbara Pinot, Paso Robles Zinfandel, Argentinean Malbec, Spanish Rioja, Italian Barbera or Chianti. There are a thousand others that will fit and work, but if you see any of these on the menu… you're probably going to be fine.

You are also looking at price. Here are the secrets that only wine industry people know. Most wine by the bottle is marked up between 100-400%. The game is to find the best value… the one closest to 100% and furthest from 400%.

You'll have more luck in the middle-high price ranges. The restaurant management has already decided they won't sell a bottle for less than a certain amount, so the lowest priced bottle gets automatically marked up to that amount… even if it costs far less than the next lowest priced bottle. For instance, I've seen cheap bottles marked up more than 800% just to get them up to an acceptable per glass price. If the restaurant or bar gets a great deal, they are not passing savings along to customers. So you want to get up past that first tier if you can, where the gains start to get more marginal.

The highest priced wines do tend to be a good "value" – but this depends on your definition of value and of course, the level of quality in the restaurant. Let's assume you're not at the best steakhouse in any of the top 10 markets in the US. (If you are… just ask the sommelier to pick a well-structured medium bodied red and then relax, you did your job).

Let's assume you're at a mid-tier restaurant that may or may not be a chain and definitely does not have a sommelier on staff (the manager of small restaurants is usually the next best thing, FYI). You want to figure out the median price on the menu, and then go for the bottle just above the median that's from the regions I mentioned. I've found some incredible values while using this method.

If you want, you can casually mention that you read a great book and it told you to pick the wine you've just selected… it won't be a complete fabrication of the truth, and it'll make you look credible enough to bully everyone's doubting palates into submission.

HOW DO I SPOT A QUALITY WINE?

Most people who buy an expensive wine assume they are getting higher quality. While there's undoubtedly some truth to this assumption, once you decide on the level at which you're investing in a bottle ($2-$11, $12-25, $26-50, or $50+) then how do you tell for sure which wines are better than their price peers? That's where some knowledge of the basic wine regions, varietals, laws, and major producers will help you. On almost every bottle of wine are three key identifiers to help you deduce what's inside the glass: Region, Winemaker, and if it's a New World style wine… the Varietal (grape).

Now there's also the year, and in certain cases there are other signifiers, for instance with Port you'll need to learn what ruby, tawny, vintage and reserve mean, with Sherry you'll need to learn what Fino and Amontillado mean, German style wines and most sparkling wines will tell you about the sweetness level if you know the lingo, and you may see other interesting signifiers like "late vintage" or "premier cru" or "cuvee prestige."

In your case, you're looking for the region, the grape, and then if it's an old world wine or new world wine.

In general, what I always tell people is you are looking for the region and/or varietal that fits your palate, and then if all else is equal, price will start to actually matter.

There is usually a big difference between a $5 and a $15 bottle; but I believe you'll find quality begins a marginal return on the dollar between $18-$45. Then after about $50 per bottle, you're getting into wine with either established history of a consistent product or a cult following (you'd be surprised how many rock stars and celebrities exist in the wine world). You may also be dabbling with aged wine after that cash threshold, which requires a lot more study than I'm able to give you at the moment.

Here is a list of the most expensive wines by average price... just in case you want to know:

Wine Name	Avg. Price (USD)	Max. Price (USD)
Domaine de la Romanee-Conti Romanee-Conti Grand Cru, Cote de Nuits, France	$13,181	$36,949
Henri Jayer Cros Parantoux, Vosne-Romanee Premier Cru, France	$7,759	$15,656
Egon Muller-Scharzhof Scharzhofberger Riesling Trockenbeerenauslese, Mosel, Germany	$7,255	$13,302
Domaine Leflaive Montrachet Grand Cru, Cote de Beaune, France	$5,893	$10,032
Joh. Jos. Prum Wehlener Sonnenuhr Riesling Trockenbeerenauslese, Mosel, Germany	$5,415	$14,260
Domaine Leroy Musigny Grand Cru, Cote de Nuits, France	$5,353	$16,485
Domaine Georges & Christophe Roumier Musigny Grand Cru, Cote de Nuits, France	$5,075	$13,835
Domaine de la Romanee-Conti Montrachet Grand Cru, Cote de Beaune, France	$4,672	$10,974
Domaine Jean-Louis Chave Ermitage Cuvee Cathelin, Rhone, France	$3,805	$7,614
Henri Jayer Echezeaux Grand Cru, Cote de Nuits, France	$3,479	$15,000

WHICH IS THE BEST WINE BRAND?

This depends on who you ask. There are top wine growing regions for each grape or style. There are top growers within each top-growing region. There are top winemakers in each growing region. And sometimes the people who build up a great brand move to other brands and there's a perceived value that isn't there anymore.

The first attempt to codify which wines were best, was done in the now famous 1855 Bordeaux list from Louis Napoleon.

The Official 1855 Classification of Napoleon III
(Modern names are in parentheses)

FIRST-GROWTHS
PREMIERS CRUS
Château Lafite Rothschild Pauillac
Château Latour Pauillac
Château Margaux Margaux
Château Haut-Brion Pessac, Graves (since 1986, Pessac-Leognan)

SECOND-GROWTHS
DEUXIEMES CRUS
Château Mouton-Rothschild (became a first-growth in 1973) Pauillac
Château Rausan-Segla (Rauzan-Segla) Margaux
Château Rauzan-Gassies Margaux
Château Léoville Las Cases St.-Julien
Château Léoville Poyferré St.-Julien
Château Léoville Barton St.-Julien
Château Durfort-Vivens Margaux
Château Gruaud-Larose St.-Julien
Château Lascombes Margaux
Château Brane-Cantenac Cantenac-Margaux (Margaux)
Château Pichon-Longueville-Baron Pauillac
Château Pichon Longueville Comtesse de Lalande (Pichon-Longueville-Lalande) Pauillac
Château Ducru-Beaucaillou St.-Julien
Château Cos-d'Estournel St.-Estèphe
Château Montrose St.-Estèphe

THIRD-GROWTHS
TROISIEMES CRUS
Château Kirwan Cantenac-Margaux (Margaux)
Château d'Issan Cantenac-Margaux (Margaux)
Château Lagrange St.-Julien
Château Langoa Barton St.-Julien
Château Giscours Labarde-Margaux (Margaux)
Château Malescot-St.-Exupéry Margaux
Château Cantenac-Brown Cantenac-Margaux (Margaux)
Château Boyd-Cantenac Margaux
Château Palmer Cantenac-Margaux (Margaux)
Château La Lagune Ludon (Haut-Médoc)
Château Desmirail Margaux
Château Calon-Ségur St.-Estephe
Château Ferrière Margaux
Château Marquis-d'Alesme-Becker Margaux

FOURTH-GROWTHS
QUATRIEMES CRUS
Château St.-Pierre St.-Julien
Château Talbot St.-Julien
Château Branaire-Ducru St.-Julien
Château Duhart-Milon Rothschild Pauillac
Château Pouget Cantenac-Margaux (Margaux)
Château La Tour Carnet St.-Laurent (Haut-Médoc)
Château Lafon-Rochet St.-Estèphe
Château Beychevelle St.-Julien
Château Prieuré-Lichine Cantenac-Margaux (Margaux)
Château Marquis de Terme Margaux

FIFTH-GROWTHS
CINQUIEMES CRUS

Château Pontet-Canet Pauillac
Château Batailley Pauillac
Château Haut-Batailley Pauillac
Château Grand-Puy-Lacoste Pauillac
Château Grand-Puy-Ducasse Pauillac
Château Lynch-Bages Pauillac
Château Lynch-Moussas Pauillac
Château Dauzac Labarde (Margaux)
Château Mouton-Baronne-Philippe (Château d'Armailhac after 1989) Pauillac
Château du Tertre Arsac (Margaux)
Château Haut-Bages-Libéral Pauillac
Château Pédesclaux Pauillac
Château Belgrave St.-Laurent (Haut-Médoc)
Château Camensac (Château de Camensac) St.-Laurent (Haut-Médoc)
Château Cos-Labory St.-Estèphe
Château Clerc-Milon Pauillac
Château Croizet-Bages Pauillac
Château Cantemerle Macau (Haut-Médoc)

The Judgment of Paris

If you've seen "Bottle Shock," you may be familiar with the now infamous "Judgment of Paris" in 1978 in which Napa Valley wines were judged by French wine snobs to be better than French wines (mainly Bordeaux reds and Burgundian whites). These blind tastings have been retried again and again… with the same general outcome. Here are the wines that have won those tastings:

CABERNET SAUVIGNON VS. BORDEAUX		Origin
Rank	Wine	
1	Stag's Leap Wine Cellars	USA
2	Château Mouton-Rothschild	France
3	Château Montrose	France
4	Château Haut-Brion	France
5	Ridge Vineyards Monte Bello	USA
6	Château Leoville Las Cases	France
7	Heitz Wine Cellars Martha's Vineyard	USA
8	Clos Du Val Winery	USA
9	Mayacamas Vineyards	USA
10	Freemark Abbey Winery	USA
CALIFORNIA CHARDONNAYS VS. BURGUNDY		
1	Chateau Montelena	USA
2	Meursault Charmes Roulot	France
3	Chalone Vineyard	USA
4	Spring Mountain Vineyard	USA
5	Beaune Clos des Mouches Joseph Drouhin	France
6	Freemark Abbey Winery	USA
7	Batard-Montrachet Ramonet-Prudhon	France
8	Puligny-Montrachet Les Pucelles Domaine Leflaive	France
9	Veedercrest Vineyards	USA
10	David Bruce Winery	USA

A colloquialism in the wine industry holds that "all palates end in Burgundy" which means no matter where you start or how long you try... if you are actually attempting to grow your sensibility in wine you'll end up loving Burgundy's Pinot Noirs and Chardonnays. I can attest my palate has made this loop. But it's not like I always choose a Pinot over a great Rhone blend, or Chardonnay over a dry Riesling.

WHICH COUNTRY PRODUCES THE BEST VALUE WINES?

Assuming you're looking at bank-for-buck "value," usually the country that is up-and-coming will have the best value. For instance, you might get an outstanding Cabernet from Chile or Argentina for $12-20 just because it doesn't have the Napa or Bordeaux brand value (yet). Recently I've been getting great value from Hungarian reds. In 2004, it would have been Malbec from Argentina. In 1998 it would have been Australian Shiraz. In 1978 it would have been Napa Valley. You get the idea. In general, you will be rewarded for being adventurous with your palate.

If you're talking about true overall monetary value, you are probably looking for aged Burgundy, Bordeaux, Napa Cabs, and in some cases aged Piedmonte Italians (Barbaresco, Barolo, Barbera). If you're looking to collect, you'll probably want to talk to a wine broker (yes, they're just like stock brokers for wine).

WHAT ARE THE MOST COMMON FAULTS FOUND IN WINE?

By sheer volume, probably the most common "fault" or "flaw" is flabbiness. Just general boringness in the acid or mouthfeel that comes standard in bulk wines like Yellow Tail or Charles Shaw. By necessity, these bulk wines have to create a consistency in their product, and so they add, subtract and modify their wines based on their formula for success. This means every bottle of Yellow Tail tastes like every other bottle of Yellow Tail. While this creates consistency, it also erases complexity. Again, you might find it is a perfect introduction for you, and if so, enjoy! Just know there's more to explore when and if you are ready. Heck, there's even a range to bulk wines!

Outside of over-produced wine, the most common faults in a bottle are usually caused by human error somewhere along the supply chain. I'll name them in a minute, but basically if you smell or taste anything moldy, mousy, gamey, sulfuric or vinegary, you might have a bottle with one of the many faults that can occur along the way from the vineyard to your table. If this is the case, take it back to the store and get your money back… they have a way of charging bad bottles back to the distributor.

However, if you're interested in sleuthing your way to a definitive answer to the name of your wine's problem, here are the most common faults:

Oxidized Wine, sometimes called "maderized"

Oxidization is the most common fault because wine breaks down chemically when exposed to Oxygen. I'll spare you the hard science, but essentially catalysts in the wine become oxidized if they are not bonded with another agent, which is why sulfur dioxide is introduced... one of the many reasons sulfites end up in your wine. Your wine changes aroma (and even appearance) from the moment you open a bottle and expose it to air. You can tell you've got oxidized wine if it smells or tastes like vinegar or sometimes cooked walnuts.

Often people ask me how long you can keep an open bottle before it goes bad (becomes oxidized). I tell people you have about 24 good hours from the time you pop that cork before you need to start worrying (excluding bubbly, which will be boring in a couple of hours if left uncovered). Wine preservers can extend the life of a regular bottle for another day or two; but if it's been open for a week, it's now cooking vinegar.

Cork Taint, sometimes called "TCA"

Basically this is a mold that grows either on the inside of barrels or cork. It creates earthy, musty, moldy flavors and aromas you might find in a dank old basement wherein a wet dog has been chewing on wet newspaper.

According to Andrew Waterhouse, professor of wine chemistry at UC Davis, you can pour tainted wine into a bowl with a sheet of plastic wrap, whereby the TCA will be attracted to the polyethylene and thus sifted from your wine. I cannot confirm or deny this to be true, but I'll try it next time I come across a corked bottle I can't just take back to whence it came and exchange it for money or more wine.

Brettanomyces, commonly known as "the Bretts" or "phenolic taint"

Brettanomyces is a yeast. It creates some funky smells and tastes like band-aid, horse manure, and rancid cheese or bacon fat. What's weird about this yeast is that brewers of Belgian Style trappist ales often include it on purpose.

Sulfitic

If it smells or tastes like a struck match or rotten eggs, you have a sulfur surplus in your wine. Try decanting it for half an hour.

Tartrate Crystals or "Sediment"

These are mineral deposits usually forming in unfiltered wines (often around the cork). They are harmless, clear (though they can be stained red), and naturally formed by potassium salt from tartaric acid. Remarkably, the bulk of commercial tartrates come from the wine industry, so if you've ever used cream of tartar, you've used a wine byproduct. Neat, huh?

WHAT MAKES ONE WINE MORE EXPENSIVE THAN ANOTHER?

Mostly reputation. Usually price increases when you begin combining any of the following traits: smaller batches, well-known terroir or regionality, a respected winemaker or brand, consistent quality from year to year, and increasingly the marketing or advertising efforts of new world wines.

Keeping and Serving Wine

HOW SHOULD I OPEN A WINE BOTTLE?

If the wine has a cork, you'll want a corkscrew – although there are some non-traditional methods for opening wine bottles without a corkscrew. You'll want to remove the paper, tin, or wax wrapper that seals the cork. Then you'll want to insert and twist the "worm" end of the corkscrew so it lines up as parallel as possible to the neck of the bottle. Then use whichever type of lever has been added to assist you. The old-fashioned way involves simple pulling the cork up with force, this can be tricky and usually involves holding the bottle awkwardly between your legs or feet while pulling the cork.

If you're opening bubbly, you'll want to remove the tin or paper, then twist and loosen the cage that holds the cork to the lip of the bottle. Keep a thumb over the cork while you hold the bottle at a 45degree angle. Press and hold the cork while you twist the bottom of the bottle counterclockwise. As you twist, begin slowly pulling the cork away from the bottle, with your hand fully grasping the neck and cork. In a few small turns, you should feel the cork wanting to jump off of the bottle. Be careful, the cork is under many atmospheres of pressure and can break glasses or severely injure someone if it were to escape you.

There is a ceremonious way to open a champagne bottle called "sabrage," in which the neck of the bottle is struck by the back end of a sabre, using the aforementioned pressure from the bottle to crack the ring around the lip of the neck, sending the cork and a ring of glass flying and forcefully opening your bottle.

This tradition comes from the days of Napoleon, when Madame Clicquot would be wooed by French soldiers with acts of bravado such as this.

It can be done cleanly and smoothly; but if not done perfectly it can send glass shards into the bottle, so you want to be pretty careful with your swordsmanship if this is the way you want to go with opening your champagne.

HOW LONG CAN YOU KEEP A WINE ONCE IT IS OPENED?

Most wine is meant to be drunk within 24-48 hours of being opened. If you use a wine saving pump or spray or other device, you might be able to squeeze another day or two out of the bottle; but really not any longer.

IN WHAT SORT OF GLASS SHOULD I BE SERVING WINE?

In all seriousness, the shape of the wine glass actually does make a difference in how you perceive a wine. I suggest you try this with your next bottle, set up a few different types of glasses (ex. mason jar, standard wine glass, plastic cup) with the same wine. Try smelling them in quick succession and see if any of them jump out at you.

The curved glass traps aromas or vapors and creates a sort of funnel for your olfactory senses.

Big wide glasses are usually reserved for big expressive wines that need a lot of surface area to "open up." Think of your big glass as a smaller version of a decanter.

WHAT'S THE BEST TEMPERATURE FOR SERVING WINE?

Most reds should be between 65-72 degrees, so slightly cooler than room temperature. Whites (including bubbly) can be served between 55-65 degrees, but do tend to be served too cold in general.

I suggest keeping your wines in a cool closet if you don't have a precise climate control wine fridge (I don't), and then popping the whites in a fridge for 2 hours before dinner, reds only 30 minutes before dinner. Imagine you are trying to keep reds at cellar or cave temperature, and whites you want to feel like they just came out of a cold stream by your fancy cave. How many wine snobs would tell you that?

I AM HAVING FRIENDS OVER FOR DINNER. HOW MUCH WINE DO WE NEED?

This depends on your friends and the dinner, of course. A bottle of wine will provide four glasses of wine (roughly) so you probably want to have 1 bottle per hour per 2 guests, giving each guest two glasses per hour if desired. So if you have 8 people around a table, you'll want 4 bottles per hour to be safe. I usually just divide the number of guests in half and buy that number of bottles.

HOW MANY BOTTLES OF WINE ARE IN A CASE?

A dozen, just like eggs.

HOW DO I REMOVE RED WINE SPILLS FROM CARPET?

Get hardwood floors! My lady swears by Wine-Away. Since you may not have that lying around, here's the blunderbuss approach of all the things I've tried or heard of.

Step 1. Get a damp sponge, lightly BLOT the stain to remove the top layers of the liquid.

Step 2. Mix 1 TBSP dishwasher liquid, 1 TBSP white vinegar, and 2 cups of warm water. Blot it onto the stain with one towel, and use a dry towel to pull it up. Do this three times.

Step 3. Pour salt onto the stain, let it sit for 8 hours, then scoop up the salt with a spoon. Vacuum the spot and it should be good as new.

Tasting Wine

WHAT IS WINE MADE OF?

I often get asked if there are actual blueberries, or sticks of butter, or tobacco in the wine. If you've ever had a flavored beer, it makes sense to ask. But no, in general, wine is made entirely from grapes.

The postcard version of wine production is that grapes are grown, harvested, crushed, fermented, aged (or not) and then bottled and shipped to wherever you procure it for your table. I'll gladly give you more on the production of wine in Chapter 6. That's enough for now.

WHAT'S THE BEST PROCESS FOR TASTING WINE?

Swirl, smell, look. Then swirl, smell, taste, breathe… repeat. I'll give you more detail in the next chapter.

Are you ready to get out your glasses and start to taste?

Chapter Five - L is for Love

How to Love the Wine in your glass

"Wine is one of the most civilized things in the world and one of the most natural things of the world that has been brought to the greatest perfection, and it offers a greater range for enjoyment and appreciation than, possibly, any other purely sensory thing."

Ernest Hemingway

The experience of tasting wine begins with picking a wine (or having one picked for you). Because this often gives people the sweats and shame, the sensual experience in wine can start out as a traumatic emotional experience. With your new Palate Identity Profile, you'll easily be able to avoid this by Asking for what you want. Let's assume you've now got a wine or two in front of you to try... how do you enjoy the experience?

The first step is to clear your pre-judgments. If you can, ignore the wine snob standing behind the bar who is trying to impress you with meaningless words about what you should smell or taste. Let them deal with their own anxiety in whatever way they want, you're here for the fun of an ancient and beautiful alcohol delivery system.

Clear your pre-judgments before you pick up the glass and remind yourself that your palate is the only one that matters. You get to have a life where you enjoy every glass of wine that is served to you.

I promise, if you do this one step, you will find something to enjoy about almost every glass you encounter. I do, and I've never looked back.

The second step is to do the traditional Swirl, Smell, Sip method.

Swirling the wine is fun. It also serves a purpose. Basically you are waking up the wine, letting it stretch, and you'll notice the "bouquet" of aromas intensifies as you swirl it. Try this: smell the wine before you swirl it, then immediately after you swirl it. You'll quickly be able to pick up more aromas than the first smell.

When you do go to smell your wine, breathe deeply while you stick your nose deeply into the glass, don't be bashful. In this hedonistic style of tasting, you are not trying to forcibly identify aromas. You are just asking yourself, "do I enjoy these aromas?" If you allow yourself to relax and take in the aromas, there's a chance your olfactory sense will effortlessly recall sensory memories you've long forgotten.

Whenever I smell a Viognier, I'm transported across spacetime to fields of lavender I once encountered near Cannes, France when I was 19 and just beginning to explore the world. These sensational memories are ten times more fun and valuable to me (and to your wine snob friends, if they're honest) than simply stating, "this smells like lavender and jasmine."

Only if a specific aroma jumps out at you should you be worried about shouting out what you smell. To me, this is an extremely personal and intimate moment that you have a right to keep private or share as you wish.

A quick aside about the visual coloring of the wine.

Most people will tell you that you can get a lot of information just by looking at your glass. This is true in the technical approach in that you can learn hints about age, viscosity, alcohol content, barrel aging and maybe even a ballpark grape varietal... but I would humbly argue that it takes a breadth of experience with different wines for this to be overly useful.

For now, when you look at a wine, you are looking for 3 things:

1. The speed and width of the "Legs" or "Tears" or rivulets of the wine on the side of your glass after you swirl... thicker means more alcohol.

2. The color gradient in your wine. The darker your wine, the more full-bodied it should be. If your wine starts out violet and ends up brickish red on the rim, it has likely aged. If your wine starts out opaque and ends up opaque, it is likely to be younger. If it is light all the way through, it is simply a light-bodied wine and not meant to age more than a few years.

3. White wine that is more brown-golden has been aged, probably in oak, and probably "sur lie" or "on the lees." Lees are essentially the fallen out remains of the microscopic yeast from fermentation. If you see gold, you have a white that is going to have some complex profiles likely to involve nutty, caramel, toasty, bready, or buttery characteristics.

After you swirl and smell a few times to warm up your olfactory senses, it's time to sip. Congratulations! You got to the part where you get to drink some alcohol!

There's no wrong way to sip, but there is definitely a method to getting the most out of the experience. As long as you're swirling, smelling and then sipping, you're not likely to screw up. Just in case, here's the method I'd recommend.

Immediately after smelling the wine, sip a medium mouthful, swish it around to coat the entire surface area of your mouth, then if you can without dribbling, try to breathe in some air. You'll notice that the tastes and aromas

101

change and expand with a little oxygen. Feel the weight of it. Does it feel more like water, coffee, or milk? Does it feel hot or cool? Does it make your tongue pucker up, or does it make your mouth water? Believe it or not, this is often called the "mouthfeel" and it refers to the acidity, viscosity and alcohol content of the wine.

Truth be told, our tongue is a pretty rudimentary tool. It's evolved to help you discern 5 basic qualities: sweetness, bitterness, sourness, saltiness, and umami (savory meatiness). So in the action of sipping, you're really not getting much from the tongue except, "Mmmm, this is good," or "Eh, this is too (sweet, sour, bitter) for me." But if you see the action of sipping as also a tactile action in feeling the wine, you'll get more out of the experience.

After you swallow, breath in through your nose and you'll notice that you can taste the wine in the back of your throat. Yes, you have receptors even in your throat.

I've included a tasting chart for you to print out and use at your next tasting.

I gave you room for two glasses because I like to do tastings of two different wines at the same time, if possible.

This makes comparison and contrast more distinguishable and fun.

You want to write down what you like... not what you're supposed to like. The grape, region, and winemaker are worth knowing. Then rate it based on your experience, and make sure you've included all of your senses in the experience.

I've also included here a copy of the Sommelier tasting guide, as an example of the difference in technical tasting vs. hedonistic tasting.

Certified Sommelier Tasting Exam
White Wine Tasting Grid

Name _____

Fill in the correct lettered space completely!

AROMA / FLAVOR ASSESSMENT

#			Mark ONE to THREE boxes
1	Fruit Generic Descriptor:	a) Apple/Pear b) Stone Fruit c) Citrus Fruit d) Tropical Fruit	[a] [b] [c] [d]
2	List Specific descriptor(s):		
3	Non-fruit Generic Descriptor:	a) Floral b) Spice c) Herbs d) Other	Mark ONE to THREE boxes [a] [b] [c] [d]
4	List Specific Descriptor(s):		
5	Earth/Mineral Generic Descriptor:	a) Little/None b) Stone/Minerals c) Earth/Mushrooms	Mark ONE to TWO boxes [a] [b] [c]
6	List Specific Earth/Mineral Descriptor(s):		
7	Use of Oak:	a) No Evidence of Oak b) Matured in Oak	Mark only ONE box [a] [b]
8	List Specific Wood Descriptor(s):		

STRUCTURE ASSESSMENT

#			Mark no more than two adjacent boxes
9.	Sugar	a) Dry b) Off Dry c) Medium Sweet d) Sweet e) Dessert	[a] [b] [c] [d] [e]
10.	Acid	a) Low b) Medium minus c) Medium d) Medium Plus e) High	[a] [b] [c] [d] [e]
11.	Alcohol	a) Low b) Medium minus c) Medium d) Medium Plus e) High	[a] [b] [c] [d] [e]
12	Finish	a) Short b) Medium minus c) Medium d) Medium Plus e) Long	[a] [b] [c] [d] [e]

INITIAL AND FINAL CONCLUSION

#			Mark only ONE box per line below
13.	Climate:	a) Cool b) Moderate c) Warm	[a] [b] [c]
14.	Style:	a) Old World b) New World	[a] [b]
15.	Grape(s):	a) Chardonnay b) Sauvignon Blanc c) Chenin Blanc d) Riesling e) Viognier f) Pinot Gris/Grigio	[a] [b] [c] [d] [e] [f]
16.	Country:	a) France b) Italy c) United States d) Australia e) Germany f) New Zealand	[a] [b] [c] [d] [e] [f]
18.	Vintage:	a) 1995-2000 b) 2001-2003 c) 2004-2006 d) 2007-2008	[a] [b] [c] [d]

If you want to learn more about the chemical processes of tasting, I'll point you in the direction of some classes and books that will help you get deeper knowledge.

Holding the glass

Some people will tell you to hold the glass in certain ways. Just remember your hand is warm, so if you want to heat up your wine, hold it by the bowl of the glass. If you want to keep it cold, hold it by the stem.

Chapter Six - *A is for Adventure*

How to plan your Adventure through new wine regions and

grapes

"No poem was ever written by a drinker of water."

Homer

Now, it's time to get Adventurous!

First, find yourself some new grapes to love. Take the first test of your new tasting skills and find yourself a wine bar/boutique near your home with a wine list. Saddle up to the bar and ask for an adventure. Tell the bartender your palate profile characteristics and ask them to pour you a taste of something new and unique.

This is the easiest way to explore the world because bartenders will honor your palate preference and pour something unique in varietal or region. Having been this bartender myself many thousand times, I can tell you, this is the best part of the job. You are making someone's day by asking for an adventure.

HOMEWORK

Befriend the bartenders at 3 wine boutiques or bars in your nearest town, and you'll start to get a good idea of what's out there.

You may find that Pinotage is actually more your favorite than Bordeaux this way. And then you'll find that a great Cabernet Franc actually suits you even more.

Bars/restaurants are better for you in this stage than going to a liquor store and trying to pick your wine off the shelves.

Most of your local grocery/liquor stores have a TERRIBLE-TO-MEDIOCRE selection of wine with only a handful of marginally interesting wines.

Here's why: Your grocery store is part of a huge chain where the sheer amount of product needed to fill shelves would rule out any smaller suppliers of wine. Given time, this vector produces dressed-up bulk wines, and then bulkifies all the decent mid-range wines.

Your liquor store is tied up with a specific distributor with a large book of wines they need to sell. They don't take risks and they do a lot of market research which means they sell to the middle... to the mediocre. So you end up with homogeneous mediocrity. You can find diamonds in the rough at both... but it'll cost you.

Go to little boutique wine shops/bars and you'll be working with smaller brands and lesser-known regions. Given time, this vector creates wines that must entice you back with unique quality. Little boutiques and bars also have an on-site curator who is selecting wines every week or two. You're almost guaranteed a wine you've never heard of before. Price also matters a lot less here. You're getting solid wine at every price point at small-time establishments.

Restaurants can run the gamut... but the bigger the chain, the closer to the grocery store you're going to get.

Next, there is a winery near you... although you may not know it. There are wineries in all 50 United States and in most countries between the 30th and 50th parallels. I have helped plant vines in North Texas where summers are too hot and winters should be too cold; and yet the vines grew and produced heartily. Find the wine region closest to you and call a winemaker to ask about their tasting hours and wine club.

They will have a wine club, and they will welcome you to a free tasting if you're interested in joining their club. Wine clubs are amazing. You can get incredible (and often very small batch) wine sent directly from your local winery a few times per year for a nominal fee that often works out to great discounted deals for you.

Then go to the tasting room nearest you and just ask questions as much as you can. You will love this experience because it's like finding a secret garden just over your backyard fence. You'll want to take everyone you know to this new and fantastic place you've found. They'll say yes. It'll change your life and the way you look at the area around you.

Next, plan your trip to any of the world's top regions.

According to USA TODAY readers, here are the top 10 wine regions to visit:

Alentejo, Portugal

Okanagan Valley, British Columbia

Maipo, Chile

Marlborough, New Zealand

Croatia

Napa Valley, Calif.

Tuscany, Italy

Oregon

Hunter Valley, Australia

Virginia

Did you notice how not a single French region made this list? Nor Spanish, nor Argentinean, nor African... yikes USA TODAY readers, what were you thinking? Virginia is very nice, but it beats ALL French valleys? I thought I'd show you another example of how subjective wine is, even given a larger sample size. Now, back to you and me.

I can vouch for several regions that did not make this ridiculous list.

Dale's Additional List of Regions Not to Miss

Bordeaux, France

Piedmont, Italy

Mendoza, Argentina

Central Coast, California, USA

Rhone Valley/Provence, France

Rheingau, Germany

Lake Chelan, Washington, USA

Loire Valley, France

Vienna/Danube Valley, Austria

The Catalonia Cava routes, Spain

Burgundy, France

Douro Valley, Portugal

Cape Town/Stellenbosch, South Africa

St. Emilion, Bordeaux, France

When you go to these regions, remember this universal truth: the best tasting experiences are never in the town square. So if you go to the town center of Santa Barbara, Bordeaux, or Porto, just know that the better wine is up on the side of a hill somewhere nearby. The town's center may be convenient (and certainly worthwhile); but the best tasting rooms are at the vineyard or winemaker's facility (or home).

Part of the advantage of going to the vines is you get to see the vines. There is nothing better in the world than tasting wine in a vineyard.

Another big advantage is that you can often meet the winemaker or grower (sometimes you may even meet the entire family, as I have many times), and ask questions all day of a person who loves to talk about wine more than anything else in life... because almost nobody ends up in the wine industry who doesn't LOVE wine.

If you are persistent and charming enough, you will eventually be given complimentary tastes of the special bottle that is hidden under the bar or behind the fridge. Using this method of earnest interest, I've been invited in to taste wine DIRECTLY FROM THE BARRELS. I've seen 1000 year-old caves in the basement of a family's home.

I've tasted dusty, unlabeled bottles from cellars of families with royal lineage. You can't underestimate the power of wanting an adventure and being ready for it when it happens.

The more you do this, the more you will learn and love the experience of wine. Again, ask about wine clubs… you might be able to get into some great arrangements for wine to show up at your front door each year.

In summary, to plan your adventure you need to know your Palate, Ask questions, and open yourself up to Loving the experience in front of you.

Chapter Seven - *T is for Technical*

How to Understand the Technical Stuff

"A man will be eloquent if you give him good wine."

Ralph Waldo Emerson

By now, you may have visited a vineyard and discovered that there's a lot to the process. You might also be enticed to try your hand at growing some vines or fermenting some grape juice in your garage. If that's you, and you need to dive in, I understand. I've been there. It's how my father ended up with Cabernet Sauvignon growing in his back yard.

This chapter is for you if you're curious about the "How To" of wines. I'll give you successive levels of the process, but this really is a 101 book, so I'll recommend the next level of reading you should dig into from some venerable authors I respect.

The process in a nut-shell:

Grapes are grown

Grapes are harvested

Grape juice is fermented with yeast

Wine is aged and bottled

Wine is marketed, shipped, and somehow finds its way to your table

Want more detail? So did I when I started out. First stop on this education train is a vineyard where we will learn about the growing of grapes, or "viticulture." I'll do my best to give you what I find interesting and relevant, but just know that there are libraries devoted to each small section I'll address here.

Viticulture

Cabernet Sauvignon grapes during véraison in my father's backyard vineyard, in their 3rd season

CAN I GROW GRAPES IN MY BACKYARD?

Probably. Grapes grow on a grapevine, which is a weak-stemmed climber that covers more than 20 million acres on all continents except Antarctica. It has some basic nutritional requirements: Nitrogen, Phosphorous, and Potassium, along with 6 other minor nutrients. Essentially, if you properly tend grapevines, you can get them to grow almost *anywhere (*that's a big almost that depends on the word "properly"). But before you throw vines into the ground, there's a difference between growing and producing.

Vines take 3 years to produce their first real crop, and 6 years before they're considered "mature." They will produce their greatest yields between 6-20 years old, but there are century old vines that produce some really interesting wines (California old vine Zinfandel is a prominent example).

Vines go dormant after harvest and develop fairly hardy defenses against cold and frost... although in colder climates like Austria and Canada, growers are known to bury their vines during winter to protect them from frost damage. Vines are also capable of withstanding incredibly dry heat during the summers, as long as their canopies are well-managed. There are also some serious bugs and diseases that can threaten the leaves, roots, vines, and fruit, so you'll have to be vigilant with your backyard vines during the growing season – as are most grape growers.

In other words... vines are capable of growing in lots of climates, but they won't produce without lots of care (there's a lot of philosophical debate on this point, but mainly it focuses around the definition of care – everybody agrees there's lots of maintenance).

ARE DIFFERENT GRAPES REALLY THAT DIFFERENT?

If you've ever wondered what's really that different about Cabernet Sauvignon and Merlot... you're onto something. All of our winemaking grapes are very closely related, genealogically.

Nearly all winemaking grapes are from the same species, Vitis vinifera, which is native to Europe and west Asia. There are some vine species native to North America (think Concord jelly), but the grapes they produce aren't typically associated with fine wine. Although since an epidemic of the root louse phylloxera, most vines below high altitudes are now grafted onto the hardier American rootstock of Vitis Labrusca. The pneumonic I use to remember this tidbit is "American roots, European shoots."

Most differences in grapes are due to being varying subspecies (Chardonnay, Sauvignon Blanc, Syrah). There are some natural mutations (like Pinot Noir mutating into

Pinot Gris and Pinot Blanc), some cross-subspecies breeds (like Cabernet Sauvignon coming from a sexual reproduction of Sauvignon Blanc and Cabernet Franc), and then there are different clones of the same subspecies (cuttings taken from a single plant by asexual reproduction).

WHAT IS TERROIR?

This French term basically means the sum of all the area-specific parts of any given vineyard. It's like asking the question, *"What is Art?"*

The concept inspires a debate you probably don't want to wade into if you see two sommeliers arguing with words like "clay composition," "marine influence," or "Burgundian heritage."

I'll tell you my *opinion*. I like the idea of uniqueness. The sheer amount of variables of people and climate and other inputs seems to suggest that no two wines will ever be alike. However, a small region might create consistency through lineages of growers and makers, long-term consistency in climate and soil, and a developed bias for specific grapes and winemaking styles. So I think it's reasonable to suggest that selective evolutionary processes could create a uniqueness from a small region that we would interpret as a pattern significant enough to call it the region's "terroir."

However, if you put two finely crafted glasses of Pinot Noir from two distinctly different places in front of 99% of the wine-drinking world, we'd all say, "wow, can I have more?" The differences are probably there, but the discernment of the differences is a lofty goal for a small minority.

In the book *Terroir*, James E. Wilson makes the case that soil is the "soul of the vine." Of course, the slope, altitude and orientation of the hill a vine grows on are all important, but Wilson notes that what's underneath the hillside is the most important factor influencing the character of a wine.

The most common soil fractions you'll see are clay, silt, sand, minerals, rocks, and organic matter.

What matters to you is that you can begin to grasp the patterns of taste and style from general regions you are exploring. The more you taste, the more you will see the patterns, the more you will be able to understand which regions fit your palate the best.

WHAT HAPPENS AFTER GRAPES ARE HARVESTED?

Grapes are usually de-stemmed and crushed (in various ways with various levels of hierarchical value depending on the methods).

The grape juice (called "must") is then fermented by either adding yeast or cultivating natural yeast from the vineyard (yeast is a friendly microscopic bacteria).

Yeast consumes the natural sugar in the grape juice and any added sugar, producing ethyl alcohol, heat, fascinating aromas and carbon dioxide (and a very small percentage of other volatile byproducts). For dry wines, this fermentation ends when the yeast is permitted to consume 99% of the sugar in the juice. For sweet wines, this process can be stopped in a few ways leading to different levels of alcohol and residual sugar.

Wines that are red have fermented in a tank, vat, or barrel with the grape skins/stems/pits. White wines generally ferment without their skins. Rosés ferment partially with and partially without their skins. Bubbly wines undergo a second fermentation in the bottle... where the CO_2 is trapped inside the wine instead of released from the tanks or vats. As with all things, there are dozens of exceptions; but 99.9% of wine is bottled up grape juice, yeast, and time.

If you want to really dive into the chemical composition of wine, you can look into "A primer on the composition of wine" by Andrew Waterhouse, of the department of viticulture and enology at the Davis campus of University of California.

Chapter Eight - *E is for Education*

How to get more Education if you want it

"There's truth in wine, and there may be some in gin and muddy beer; but whether it's truth worth my knowing, is another question."

George Eliot

Eighty percent of people want to learn more about wine, according to a survey by Impulse Research Corp.

Learning about wine is only fun if you realize from the beginning that you will never know it all. If you can feel the freedom in that statement, then you are ready to learn more. It may seem daunting to begin any sort of directed or formal education into wine, so I've put this chapter together to give you some foresight into the unknown future.

There are basically 5 ways to learn wine – and you can use them concurrently or separately. They are all valuable in their own ways, and all types of learners can find something to match their specific needs.

You've bought this book, so you're already doing method 1... Congratulations!

EDUCATION METHODS:

1. Books, Magazines and Online Learning

2. Travel, Tasting, and Events

3. Hobbyist Classes

4. Certificate and Degree Programs

5. Growing or Fermenting Grapes

Method 1: Books, Magazines and Online Learning

Why do books, magazines and online learning go together? Because of the underwear factor... you can use these methods from the privacy of your own home (and underwear).

You can learn a lot of basics, history, vocabulary and laws from books, videos, Twitter Simultastings, food+wine magazines, and many other avenues. It's mostly safe from any snobbish ridicule, and you have total control over the beginning, middle, and end of the experience. For this reason it's a great way to quickly begin your journey. However this avenue is fundamentally lacking in the unforeseeable sensory adventure of interacting with others around a bottle, and therefore you will reach a point early in your journey where underwear learning gives you marginal rates of return.

In my journey with wine, I have found books and online learning to be particularly helpful when I wanted to dive deeply into any supplemental or cursory information. For instance, if you want to learn about wine soil, the definitive work is absolutely Terroir by James E. Wilson. If you want to learn about what happened to wine during the World Wars, you'll want to read either Wine and War or Champagne by Don and Petie Kladstrup. If you are looking for the esoteric technical mumbo-jumbo, you'll want to read The Science of Wine by Jamie Goode.

5 Books to Read
(in order of recommended progression)

Windows on the World by Kevin Zraly

The World Atlas of Wine by Hugh Johnson and Jancis Robinson

Wine and War or Champagne by Don and Petie Kladstrup

Adventures on the Wine Route by Kermit Lynch

Terroir by James E. Wilson

You can think of magazines and the web like they are the gossip column for the industry. I've found magazines and Twitter in particular are crucial for determining who are the winemaking celebrities, what they're wearing (drinking), and where they're visiting.

Believe it or not, this is extremely valuable if you want to get deeper into wine education. If you begin to recognize names from magazines on the front (or as is often the case, on the back) of your bottles, you can begin to get an even deeper understanding of what's in the bottle you're opening. There are certain Negociants who you will learn to trust for imports (based on what you know you like).

Magazines are where snobbery starts, in my opinion. When Robert Parker attempted to codify wine with the 100-point scale in the Wine Advocate, he created a monster that was probably destined to happen at some point either way. While I understand and appreciate the draw to systemize subjectivity in order to help people choose wine more intelligently... I know the 100-point system skews high on tannins and full-bodied whites, which that excludes many of the palates I've witnessed.

Of the wine magazines, Wine & Spirits is one of the few that doesn't even engage in rankings by a 100-point scale. I also prefer Spectator to Enthusiast, because essentially they are both travel and leisure magazines and Spectator spends a lot of time in fancy restaurants I'll probably never afford. And finally there's the World of Fine Wine, which is heady and intellectual. If you want to really dive in, this is a really good start.

Top 3 Magazines
(in order of recommended progression)

Wine & Spirits

Wine Spectator

The World of Fine Wine

I have learned a little from Youtube, I admit. There are some savvy winemakers out there who are using the web to talk to web citizenry in our language.

Dale's Top 3 Favorite Video Blogs
Jordan Vineyard & Winery

Wine Oh! Tv

Wes Hagen from Clos Pepe – rough, but short and insightful

If you are a blogophile, there are probably some great ones that focus specifically on your region of interest. You can learn some things from these sources, and they're often nice resources to connect with via social media.

Dale's Top 3 Favorite Wine Blogs
Madelinne Puckett, Wine Folly

Dezel Quillen, My Vine Spot

Amy Gross, VineSleuth

Method 2: Travel, Tasting, and Events

There is a certain amount of knowing that comes from having been there. Sometimes you need to go out and experience something for yourself. The books and magazines and all the fancy photos in the world can't give you a sensory experience like a vineyard or a tasting or an event. It just can't. The first time I stepped foot on a vineyard was in the Chateauneuf-du-Pape region, and I knew as soon as my sole hit soil that my soul had found a place to put down roots.

Aside from the warm fuzzy feelings that come from rows of sun-kissed vines, there is knowledge in the air around those rows. There are real people who groom the vines, who care for the soil, who tend the grapes as they ferment, and whose livelihood is profoundly altered by intimate knowledge about their product.

All of those people are within a stone's throw of a vineyard. You cannot and will not find serious wine knowledge anywhere outside of earshot of a working vineyard.

So go! I've covered this already throughout the book, so I will add that if you're not near a vineyard, find a self-respecting wine bar and go to their tastings (they all have them). What you will learn from tasting is how to taste. You'll learn more about what you like. You'll learn a little about the sub-culture of the wine market. You'll find there are lots of other people who are also dabbling a big toe in the deep waters of wine, and you may find companions along your journey.

As for events, these are usually public events like a harvest festival, a select regional tasting event, or some other kind of stunt to get you into a place of vinobusiness. The best thing to get from these types of events is an understanding of breadth. You can easily taste dozens of different wines at these events, back to back to back. How often are you afforded an opportunity to compare wines so closely together in time? This can help you deduce more quickly whether you prefer Petite Syrah over Cabernet Franc (if you like one, you probably like both, but which one cuts you deepest, maybe neither?).

Method 3: Hobbyist Classes
You might find yourself in what I'd call an informal class for hobbyists due to a special web deal like Groupon, or you might have stumbled across a class in the local "To-do" papers, or you might have been gifted a class to learn

wine with your new spouse for your honeymoon. In any case, you are in for an experience and some education.

These are usually more pointed than simple bar tastings, but they're not quite to the level of getting certifications. These kinds of classes are generally fun and experiential while still being led by a bona fide wine expert who is trying to give you some deeper technical knowledge. I've been to very good ones and I've been to some shakier ones; but they've all been valuable.

When you find yourself at one of these classes, you may be introduced to the concept of "spitting." At first it seems irrational, then you realize the skill is about wine "tasting," not wine "drinking." If you're going to remember anything from the class, you'll want to make sure you save your gulps for later in the evening. The more alcohol you consume, the less likely you are to fully experience anything after your 3rd pour.

If you like a wine, and you want to spend more time with it, ask for a new glass! The person teaching the class will appreciate your participation and will gladly give you a new glass (if it's feasible) so you can save the one you like for later. This is perfectly acceptable etiquette and I wouldn't hesitate to ask for more time or more glasses if you have paid for (or received) the class. Having been on both sides of this exchange, I can guarantee that you will be met with admiration.

I would argue that many novice wine classes are going to assume you know less than you have hopefully learned from this book. If you were to consistently take a class even a few times per year, you'd learn some good tidbits and get more comfortable in the presence of other wine lovers. Just be careful not to let the teacher shame you or disrespect your palate if it doesn't conform to his/hers. If pressed, tell them some keywords from your Palate Profile and then ask them what they like. Most people who would try to impress their palates on you are narcissists with some insecurities around their expertise. Give them an opportunity to show they know their own palate, and they'll probably forget what they were concerned about in the first place.

Method 4: Certificate and Degree Programs
This is where you get your Certified Educators, Sommeliers and Masters of Wine. If you want to get serious about serving, selling, buying, or working in the service side of wine... having a certification or degree can help vault you into better paying positions or areas of the industry.

If you've seen the excellent documentary Somm, then you have some idea of the higher intellectual levels of this world. Don't worry – they're not all terrifying and soul-crushing. Like any intellectual pursuit, you will gradually conquer levels of proficiency as you go.

The guild certifications are excellent measures of your expertise around service, history, laws, regions, and tasting. The deadline effect of a test can force you to quickly learn vast subsets of rote knowledge. However, it can take many years to prepare for even the basic levels of many guilds.

After 8 years of service experience, travel, reading and hobbyist classes, I took the first test in the Society of Wine Educators without much study except a crash course, and I failed the test by one percentage point. The second time through I studied intently for more than 6 weeks and passed... earning my Certification as a Specialist of Wine... which opened doors to writing for AmericanWineryGuide.com as a Central Coast Writer... which brought me to write this book.

If you want to go this route, I'd recommend signing up for the exam in the future, then starting a study group with friends who will undoubtedly enjoy the "free" experience of learning wine alongside you. Having compatriots along the way can help you stay accountable and upbeat... and you'll also run less of a risk of losing perspective and friendships during the process.

Below are the guilds I'd recommend, in my perception of ascending order of difficulty and prominence in the industry. The Master Sommelier and Master or Wine are the most internationally known, although there are specific certificates from each major region in the winemaking world. So if you wanted to get certified in Champagne, you could spend some time just focusing on the bubbles from France.

Guilds and Societies
Wine and Spirit Education Trust (WSET)

Society of Wine Educators (SWE)

International Sommelier Guild (ISG)

French Wine Society (FWS)

Court of Master Sommeliers (CMS)

Institute of Masters of Wine (IMW)

The university programs vary based on whether you want to primarily be involved with the grape, the juice, or the marketplace. If you want to learn viticulture, these programs will take you out to the vineyards (either on-site or through internships) where you'll get your hands dirty to go along with the classroom-based theory. If you're interested in the production process, you'll study and spend real time with tanks and fermentation. If you're interested in marketing, you'll learn the history and economics of the industry.

Many wineries and vineyards in Napa have a UC Davis grad or two running around the grounds. Same goes for Paso Robles and Cal Poly, upstate New York and Cornell, Oregon and OSU, etc. There are undergraduate and advanced studies at many of the schools below.

Here is a non-exhaustive list of universities with wine studies, in no particular order.

Universities and Degree Programs
University of California - Davis

University of Missouri

Washington State University

California State University

Oregon State University

Cornell University

Sonoma State University

California Polytechnic State University

Method 5: Growing or Fermenting Grapes
If you ask anyone in the wine industry who are the great experts in wine, nobody will look at the little letters behind a name or talk to you about a wine writer. They'll point to the experts who grow grapes and make wine. They'll point to people with dirt and grapes under their

fingernails like Stephane Derononcourt (who is self-taught), or Phillipe Melka (who has a master's degree in Enology), or Heidi Barrett (who makes some of the most highly prized wines in the world), or Merry Edwards (who is a Pinot Noir clonal scientist and genius), or Paul Hobbs (a soil nerd and marketing savant)… you get the idea.

The living, breathing, everyday nature of a winemaker's necessary expertise overshadows all the books by respected authors like Jancis Robinson or Hugh Johnson, or writing by reviewers like Robert Parker, or classes by teachers like Kevin Zraly. Those are experts, obviously, but I think they'd agree that you can't learn more quickly or profoundly than you can if you work with the grapes.

There is a difference between people who love wine as an end goal and the types of people who love the process of wine for the journey. If you truly want to learn about wine, grow some grapes, make some wine at home, or go work on a nearby vineyard.

The beauty of this is how accessible grapevines are. It's actually not too challenging to procure yourself a few grapevines for planting. It's also not too challenging to find a home winemaking kit and some juice to start experimenting with. There are some great books out there to help you, and blogs, and classes, and you'll be forced to travel to other nearby vineyards to talk to other growers, and you may take some courses to learn more... basically this method is All of the methods wrapped up into one.

If you want to get started today, I'd recommend The Backyard Vintner by Jim Law. He's pretty good at starting from zero and getting you up to speed in time to keep your vines alive and your winemaking running smoothly. This is the book my own father has used to some success with his own backyard grapevines (eight Cabernet Sauvignon vines which produced 5 gallons of wine in the 3rd leaf).

Yes, you can also call up local vineyards and ask if they need any help during harvest. Volunteer farmhands are always welcome, and you can easily strike up a sort of apprenticeship where you can exchange your enthusiasm for seasons of education and encouragement.

The point is this. Get yourself to a vineyard and really experience the vines, the soil, the fruit, the bugs, the leaves, the berries, the smells, the dew, the temperature changes, the fog, the fear, the joy, the anticipation, the hard work, the determination, the hope, and eventually... the wine. You can't learn more quickly or well.

Summary

You should have learned some things whether you skimmed this book and looked at the pictures, or if you were a good student and read every word (wow, you're a better person than I am).

If you pass this exam, please feel free to visit *www.facebook.com/DaleThomasVaughnAuthor* where you can print up your certificate of success and your Palate Identity Card.

What is your Palate Identity Profile?

What kinds of wines, grapes, and regions do you like?

What kinds of flavors and aromas do you like?

Should you ask questions when someone uses wine jargon?

Is wine good for you?

Do you know why you swirl wine?

What regions are on your bucket list to taste and/or visit?

Fundamentally, wine is the product of grape sugar and what microbial organism?

What method of wine education are you planning to pursue next?

Where is your nearest winery?

Interesting Facts To Stump the Snobs

Take these bad boys out at a party and watch everyone fall

in love with you.

In Germany, Pinot Noir is called Spatburgunder and is often made into a popular rosé called Weissherbst. It is the most widely planted red grape in Germany.

Pace Yourself! Zinfandel is legendary for its high alcohol content: 14% and higher

American Oak barrels usually impart tannic, spicy tones into red wines. French Oak barrels are less tannic and impart softer, more subtle tones into red wines.

Zinfandel and Italy's Primitivo are clones of the same variety

Chianti Vampire: Sangiovese is derived from Latin "sanguis jovis" - so when you're drinking that Chianti, you're drinking the blood of Jupiter. Makes that Chianti line from Silence of the Lambs all the more brilliant, doesn't it?

Chateauneuf-du-Pape means "New Castle of the Pope" - and is from the area around Avignon in the south of France. In 1308 a Frenchman became Pope and refused to move to Rome, thus, the new castle of the Pope. This may have led to the Western Schism and more than 100 years of French/Catholic nepotism, but he also gave us a noble wine region... so... all forgiven?

Did you know that Spain currently produces more grapes than any other country?

Muscat is often called the "grandfather grape" because scientists believe all Vinis Vinifera grapevines can be genetically traced back to Muscat. Evolution is delicious.

Chenin Blanc is called Steen in South Africa

Did You Know? The first crop of grapes to be used for wine is normally harvested after the third year, or "third leaf." But the best years are 6-20 (the French don't allow wines to be AOC until age 8).

The average time between initial budding and harvest is between 140-160 days, but can be as short as 110 days and as long as 200 days.

If you've ever had a Sauternes wine, then you have tasted wine from rotten grapes. There is a form of rot called Botrytis that, if allowed to form in certain varietals, actually produces syrupy sweet wine. This is also called "Noble Rot," and creates highly prized dessert wines exemplified by Bordeaux Sauternes and Australia's Semillon.

Eisswein, or Ice Wine, is exactly what it sounds like. Grapes are allowed to freeze on the vines, and then pressed to get a high residual sugar dessert wine. Germany, Switzerland, and New York State are known for this style of wine.

Fermentation involves roughly 30 chemical reactions, usually catalyzed by yeast. Suddenly high school chemistry class looks a whole lot more useful, doesn't it?

Sparkling wine is made with different grapes and methods all over the world, "Champagne" is the name of bubbly from the Champagne region in France. But there is also "Cava" in Spain, "Sekt" in Germany, "Spumante" in Italy, "Cremant" in the Loire Valley, and just plain "Sparkling Wine" in the US and Australia.

Madeira, once the most exported wine in the world, is cooked at temperatures above 120*F to simulate the months of un-air-conditioned ship travel it endured in the 18th and 19th centuries... giving it a caramel hue and aroma.

98% of Argentineans are descended from European immigrants, with more than half from Italy. Hence all the brilliant wine-making.

You might know Argentina's most famous red grape: Malbec; but if Malbec is king, then Torrontes is queen. The white variety is unique to Argentina and produces delicious light-bodied floral wines.

Today, Australia drinks more wine per capita than any other English-speaking nation.

Australia requires a "Best Before" date on wines not meant to have a shelf-life longer than 2 years.

Prior to the 1855 Universal Exhibition in Paris, Napoleon III requested a list of top wine chateaux from Bordeaux. The Bordeaux Classification of 1855 was created ranking vineyards based on cost... sounds smart right? Well it does not rank any vineyards from the Right

Bank, no white wine producers, and it has only changed once since its inception.

Burgundian vineyards are believed to have been introduced in 200 AD by Romans, soon to be controlled by the Catholic Church, and you guessed it, Benedictine Monks.

There are three main ways to "classify" wines: by the grape (or varietal - like Merlot, Chardonnay, etc.), by the region (like Bordeaux, Chianti, Napa, etc.), and by the vineyard (like Robert Mondavi, Chateau Lafite-Rothschild, etc.)

Dom Perignon, the monk often credited with the discovery of sparkling wine, neither invented nor perfected the process. At best, he shares that distinction with Chaptal, Brother Jean Oudart, and the widow (veuve) Clicquot.

Many of Germany's winegrowing regions are north of the 50th parallel... for comparison, the US-Canada border is on the 49th parallel)

Mount Olympus, home of Dionysus, the god of wine, is home to a vast area of bulk wine production and small boutique wineries.

If you've ever had a "Super Tuscan," you've tasted rebellion. These are vineyards that felt the rigid wine laws in Italy were cramping their styles... so instead of conform to DOC standards, these winemakers formed their own category called IGT (Indicazione Geogrifica Tipica) - the best of which we call "Super Tuscans."

Fortified Port is from the Douro Valley near Porto, Madeira is from the island of Madeira, and Sherry (or Jerez) is from Andalusia - near the city of Jerez.

There are commercial wineries in all 50 United States

The first American wines were made from native grapes around 1560 in Florida. The first European varieties were planted in Texas and New Mexico in the 1620s.

George Washington and Thomas Jefferson planted vines and made wine in the 1700s.

There are two basic lineages for grapevines: American (Vinis Labrusca), and European (Vinis Vinifera). Most winemaking grapes come from Vinifera, but because of a Vinifera-killing bug called Phylloxera, most of the wine industry comes from American roots. American roots, European Shoots...

References

1.   Dietary proanthocyanidins: occurrence, dietary intake, bioavailability, and protection against cardiovascular disease. Rasmussen SE, Frederiksen H, Struntze Krogholm K, Poulsen L. Mol Nutr Food Res [2005]

2.   Joint effect of cigarette smoking and alcohol consumption on mortality. Xu WH, Zhang XL, Gao YT, Xiang YB, Gao LF, Zheng W, Shu XO. Prev Med [2007]

3.   Mechanism by which alcohol and wine polyphenols affect coronary heart disease risk. Booyse FM, Pan W, Grenett HE, Parks DA, Darley-Usmar VM, Bradley KM, Tabengwa EM. Ann Epidemiol [2007]

4.   Renal function, cardiovascular disease risk factors' prevalence and 5-year disease incidence; the role of diet, exercise, lipids and inflammation markers: the ATTICA study. Chrysohoou C, Panagiotakos DB, Pitsavos C, Skoumas J, Toutouza M, Papaioannou I, Stefanadis C. QJM [2010]

5.   Antioxidant and cytotoxic properties of lyophilized beer extracts on HL-60 cell line. Tedesco I, Nappo A, Petitto F, Iacomino G, Nazzaro F, Palumbo R, Russo GL. Nutr Cancer [2005]

6.   Association of the availability of beer, wine, and liquor outlets with beverage-specific alcohol consumption: a cohort study. Halonen JI, Kivimaki M, Pentti J, Virtanen M, Subramanian SV, Kawachi I, Vahtera J. Alcohol. Clin. Exp. Res. [2014]

7.   Why Do I Get Headaches From Wine? Dorothy J. Gaiter and John Brecher. Wall Street Journal. April 30, 2009

Also by Dale Thomas Vaughn

Fatal Breach

Dr. Mann's Kind Folly

Connect with Me

Visit me at www.Facebook.com/DaleThomasVaughnAuthor

or

www.Twitter.com/NextGent

Your Thoughts

I love hearing from my readers so please feel free to reach me and to leave a review here on my Amazon page:

www.amazon.com/author/dalethomasvaughn

Special Offer

If you have a party coming up and you're tired of standing in the wine aisle and not knowing what to buy… If you wish you could just teleport me to the store or restaurant with you, head over to *www.facebook.com/WineSnobsAreBoring* to get access to a Wine Palate Consultation by Phone where we will hone in on if and how I can help you.

If you have purchased this book and you would like more – you really want to learn this at a fundamental level… I would love to be your solution. I offer online coursework with me personally, with video tutorials and with live events. Many of my classes start at $99, which is an unbelievable investment level to learn as much as we will cover together… and maybe a wine tasting too.

Made in the USA
Charleston, SC
20 April 2016